P9-BYM-198

The Book of Moobs

Written & Illustrated by Gray K Davis

First Published 2011

2011 Lulu.Gray K Davis. All rights reserved.
ISBN 978-1-4467-7102-0

Copyright © Gray k Davis 2011.

All rights reserved. No part of this book may
be reproduced or transmitted in any form
without the prior written permission of
the publisher.

www.bookofmoobs.com

The Book of Moobs

Written & Illustrated by Gray K Davis

Contents

Introduction

moob *noun.* blend of man and boob
plural. moobs
slang (usually in plural): a plump or untoned
breast on a man

Man Boobs or Moobs *(Vir Pectus Maximus)* have been with us since the very dawn of time. The pages of history are literally bursting at the buttons with acres of manly melons! In this one handy volume the treasured chests of our glorious forefathers are laid bare for all to see. Often derided in the modern media and sniped at by skeletal fashionistas the Man Boob is long overdue it's day in the sun.

The Book of Moobs is not only a guide book to this fascinating subject but also a celebration and owner's manual.

From Henry VIII to Churchill to Simon Cowell the great and not so good have proudly sported their 'gent jugs' through the centuries.

Kings, presidents and politicians alike have strode the corridors of power with manly confidence and a gentle bounce beneath their shirts.

This guide book will equip you with all the knowledge needed to fully understand and appreciate the beautiful bounty of Moobs that surrounds us every single day.

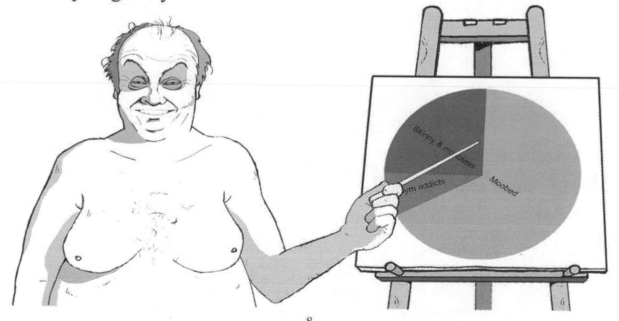

Far from being the exception Moobs are demonstrably the norm in most western countries. While the flat chested 'Beckham in the buff' look is spewed out by advertisers and 'health experts' eager to make modern men feel inadequate and therefore in dire need of purchasing their glossy products and fad diets the actual number of these 'supermen' remains tiny. Just as the fashion industry keeps western women prisoners to its unachievable 'perfect body image' so too are our men folk shamed for daring to be themselves!

Fact: Less than 6% of the adult UK male population belongs to a gym.

Fact: Less than 50% of them don't actually bother going to the damn places more than twice a year!

Fact: Women find moobs irresistible*

* What possible other explanation could there for be for the string of lovely young starlets lining up to bed millionaire film star Jack Nicholson?

Become a 'Moob Spotter'!

Understand your own 'chap baps'. Are you the proud owner of a set of 'Bunters' or perhaps a beefy pair of 'Box Buttons'? Our easy to use, fully illustrated field guide makes identification a synch. Be it a life changing revelation or just a jolly good hobby moob-spotting is all the rage - this book gives you everything that you need to know!

Find out how to keep your chaps in tip top condition with our care and maintenance section and above all learn to love your Moobs! If indeed God did create man in his own image well then . . . just think of the awesome dimensions of his divine frontage!

Amaze your friend with little known Moob facts and figures. Discover the rich and hitherto hidden history of man boobs.

While there is no definitive official medical proof of the beneficial effect of moobs on a chap's character and general demeanour the facts do seem to speak for themselves. Santa Claus, Barry White and Oliver Hardy are among the many, many jovial, cuddly and basically lovely moob bearing blokes who help to make life worth living. Are the 'moobed' among us all necessarily paragons of virtue'?

Don't be daft!

Just having a set of wobblers doesn't ensure niceness. A few notorious names leap to mind- Mussolini, Idi Amin . . Bernard Manning. It's not just having moobs it's how you use them!

Are the moob-less necessarily evil? Well of course not (at least we've not been able to prove it yet). Their flat and featureless chests are not their own fault and if anything it is our pity and understanding they deserve rather than our scorn and systematic persecution.

Chapter One: Moob Spotting

Moob Spotting is a fast growing activity practiced by nature lovers all over the world. 'Moobing' can be done almost anywhere - in the pub, high street, local car park or on a specially organised Moob Spotting holiday.

Moobing is a terrific way of connecting with nature. It can be a form of relaxation to be outside admiring moobs, or be a thrilling experience when spotting a rare pair. Not much is needed to become a moob spotter - a pair of binoculars can help while more passionate or professional moobers may want to have a telescope and of course - a good guide book.

Moob-spotting can be a good reason to get out of the house and spend time outdoors. It's an easy hobby to take up; one can start moobing almost anywhere because moobs are omnipresent! Moob-spotting is never ending because one will never have seen all moobs!

Moobing is easy to pick up, after all Moob owners are usually not among the most fleet of foot! On the other hand one can make moob-spotting as challenging as one wants. All moobs types come in a variety of sub categories and individual variations so in order to recognise them all one must learn the characteristics and tell-tale signs. Moob-spotting is a hobby that grows on a person, the more one learns the more interesting it becomes!

Basic moob-spotting equipment and preparation.

Basic moobing equipment can of course consist of no more than one's eyes but as some subjects can be un cooperative and even aggressive a pair of binoculars and a good guide book (such as this one) are recommended.

Practical things to bring on any moob-spotting trip are a hat, sun-lotion, water and some snacks, extra clothing depending on the season or time of day.

Before setting off spend some time thinking about the type and number of moobs probable at a given location. For example a day at the London marathon will offer far fewer moobing opportunities than an afternoon at your local rugby club bar.

Moob-spotting Tips.

Don't just look at moobs, there are so many other wonderful associated things to enjoy - beer bellies, shell suits and unfortunate tattoos.

Don't just look at the size of the moobs. What are their colour variations, are they bouncy or static? Is any attempt being made to conceal them or are they being flaunted proudly?

Keep a list of what moobs have been spotted and when. What was initially thought a local moob might in fact turn out to be a rare and exotic visitor!

Learn their Latin names. Some types are further subdivided in Latin than in English.

Moob-spotting is available to everybody. It is independent of age, sex, geography and financial means.

Our handy Moob identification section shows heavage both concealed by clothing and revealed in all it's glory. It's no good knowing what your quarry looks like in the buff if you can't recognise it when wrapped up!

Box Buttons

(Arca archa Puga pyga)

One of the commonest Moob types the Box Button can be found the length and breath of the country. Worn wide and high up on the chest Box Buttons are often the result of over use of the gym or regular manual labour in early life. Some times referred to as a 'barrel chest gone to seed' they blossom in early middle age and generally reach their zenith in a chap's mid to late forties.

Box Buttons

(Arca archa Puga pyga)

Notable Buttoneers: Brian Blessed, Bob Hoskins, Ray Winston, Robbie Coltrane, Meat Loaf.

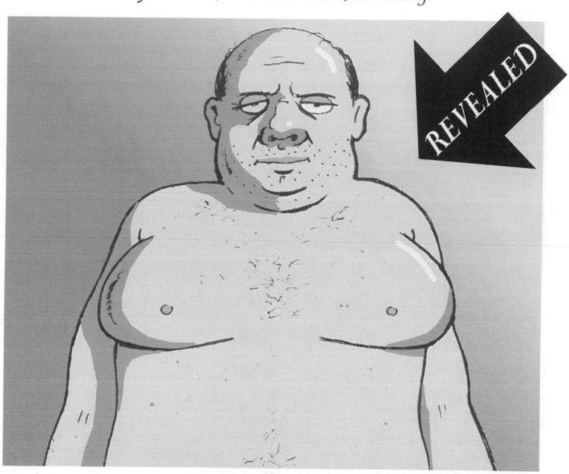

Beakers

(Rostrum Scrinium)

You don't necessarily have to be a larger lad to posses and enjoy a set of Moobs. Beakers can be found swaying away under the shirts of fellas of all sizes. Almost pendulous in appearance and low down on the chest they often occur in later life from the 50's onwards. A combination of aging skin and careful avoidance of exercise can promote Beakerism. No Saga Holiday is complete without a pair of well tanned Beakers swaying down the beach like a pair of animated saddlebags.

Beakers

(Rostrum Scrinium)

Notable Beakers: Michael Douglas,
Ian Mckellen, John Cleese.

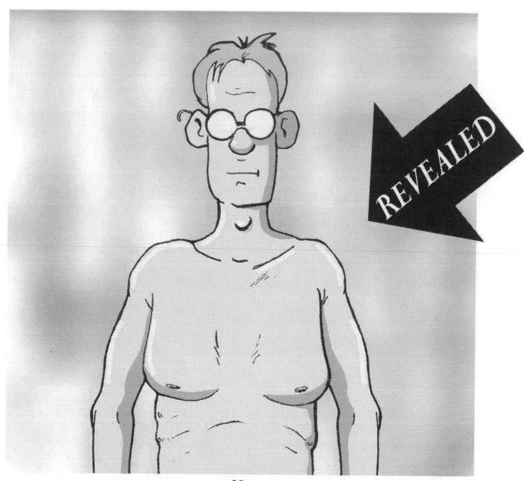

Bunters

(Pinguis schola puer scrinium)

Bunters are perhaps the sterotypical Moob most often used in film and TV. Round and curvey they are a full bodied Moob and as a rule require the owner to be of 'stocky' build. These babies are not for the skinny or half hearted. Bunters are a natural or 'given' Moob. Where as some other types of Chap-bap can be developed through lack of exercise and dedicated drinking a 'natural' Moob is something you're born with. Bunters are a classic and companions for life!

Bunters

(Pinguis schola puer scrinium)

Notable Bunters: Richard Griffiths,
Barry White, Boris Yeltsin.

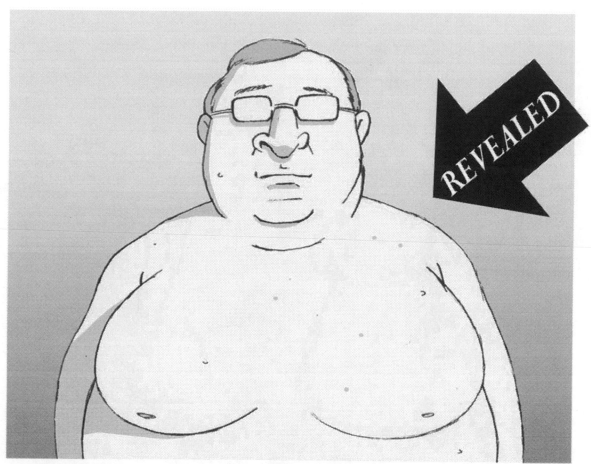

Wookies

(Vetus lupus papilla)

The Wookie aka The Hair Bear is all about fur. Basically any Moob can qualify as one so long as it is suitably hirsute. Ranging from a light downy covering to the full beaver-like pelt Wookies give hours of pleasure to owners and spectators alike. Unfortunate side effects of Wookiedom include a tendency to trap food crumbs and to form unpleasant hairy clumps when sun lotion is applied.

CONCEALED

Wookies

(Vetus lupus papilla)

Notable Wookies: Kelsey Grammer, Sean Connery
Tom Selleck, Robin Williams

The Pippin

(Vegrandis pomum papilla)

Named after the famous Cox's orange Pippin apple these are a mischievous and fun loving little Moob. Smaller in volume than some of their bouncier cousins and yet equally as impressive if used to full effect. Being wider chested and of ample torso is no bar to owning a pair of Pippins. Like a cheeky couple of bobbing tennis balls they make a real statement when worn under a tight T shirt or sweater.

The Pippin

(Vegrandis pomum papilla)

Notable Pippins: Timothy Spall, Timmy Mallet,
Matt Lucas.

Cloggies

(Maximun vir scrinium)

A Moob among Moobs! The Cloggie is a rare and illusive breed. Though to be extinct for decades until it's re emergence in Holland in 1987. No other Moob comes quite as close to being a full set of Bazoomers as this remarkable nork. If you have never witnessed a pair at first hand do not be alarmed - few have! With the advent of the internet sightings are now being flashed around the globe in minutes making instant celebrities of their owners.

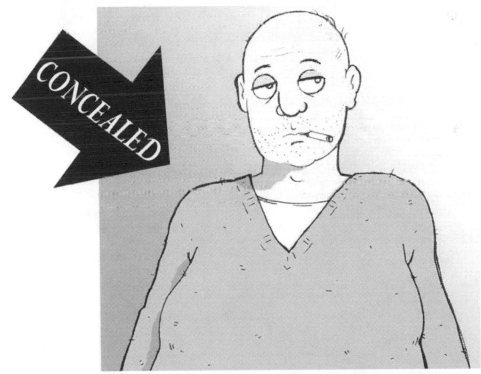

CONCEALED

Cloggies

(Maximun vir scrinium)

Notable Cloggies: None Known

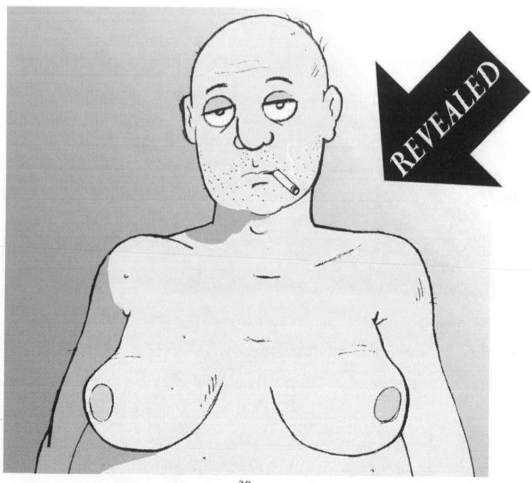

Lombards

(Insuadibilis familiaris socius)

As Tigger famously sang,

"*Bouncy, bouncy, bouncy, bouncy, fun, fun, fun, fun, fun!*"

Lombards are a close relative of the Pippin but rather more citrus in shape. High on the chest they are no bar to an athletic chap going about his sporting business. While they do bounce delightfully there is no painful flopping as can so easily occur with some of the larger Moobs. The next time you are watching a Sunday league football match keep an eye out for Lombards you won't be disappointed!

31.

Lombards

(Insuadibilis familiaris socius)

*Notable Lombardinas: Jack Black,
Jack Osbourne, Simon Cowell, Eddie Izzard.*

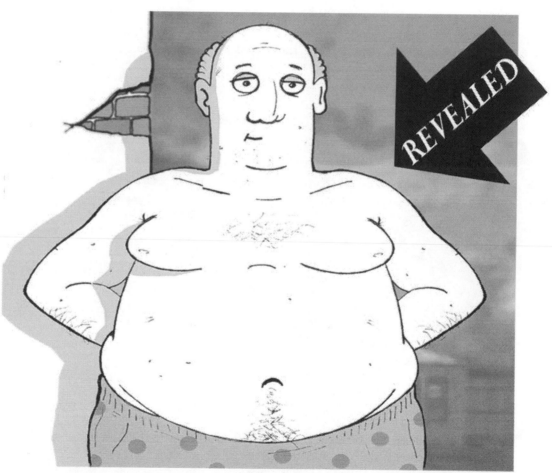

REVEALED

Lopsters

(Altus quod mugio bona)

Firstly - do not attempt to adjust your chest there is nothing wrong with it! As with so many things in nature Moobs are not necessarily symmetrical. Just as a chap's 'Man-veg' is likely to be a bit lopsided so too is his 'Heavage'. Often kept under wraps the Wun Hung Lo is more common than you may think and when on public display makes a real conversation piece!

Lopsters

(Altus quod mugio bona)

Notable Lopsters: Eamonn Holmes, Fats Domino

Sugarloafs

(Dulcis Panis)

An impressive and surprisingly common moob Sugarloafs can be found beneath the shirts of larger chaps the world over! Wide and wobbly they manage to point away from each other at angles of up to 45 degrees. Once on the move Sugarloafs can gain their own momentum and swing uncontrollably. This can be a definite plus point when performing certain forms of modern dance but a potential hazard when operating heavy machinery or tightrope walking!

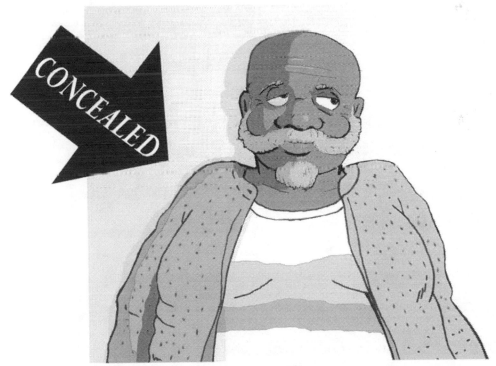

Sugarloafs

(Dulcis Panis)

Notable Loafers: Lenny Henry, Luciano Pavarotti, John Candy

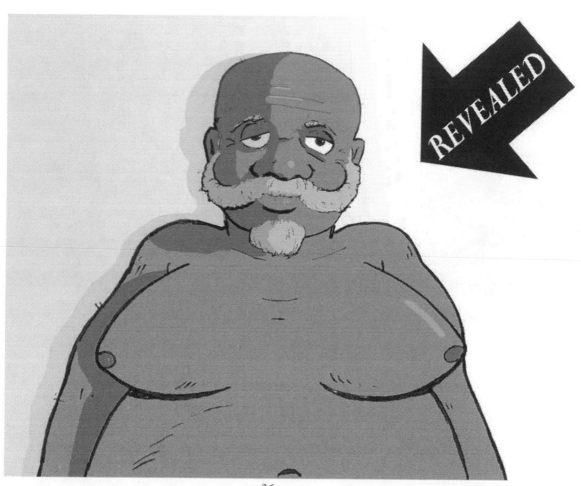

Tittoos

(Occultus tumulosus)

Astonishing as it may seem there are some gentlemen who are less than proud of their 'chap-baps'! Fortunately for these unhappy fellows there are several ways of disguising one's 'chesticles'. An effective and fashionable camouflage can be the liberal use of tattoos or 'tittoos'. Gilding the lily perhaps? We think so!

Tittoos

(Occultus tumulosus)

Notable Tittoos: Boy George, Tommy Lee . . . pretty much any old rocker on the planet.

REVEALED

McCriricks

(Vexo equus diligo)

Also known as 'coat hangers' McCriricks are a startlingly pert & lively Moob. Pointing happily skyward like a pair of playful puppy's noses they are a real head turner whenever unveiled in public. Lurking beneath a shirt or sweater McCriricks can appear deceptively petit but like any iceberg the greater part of these terrific 'fella-melons' is lurking in the depths!

McCriricks

(Vexo equus diligo)

Notable McCriricks: John McCririck (obviously),
Christopher Biggins.

Moob World Map

Moob Populations: High  Medium ⊙⊙   Low ⊙⊙

Chapter Two: Moob Fashion

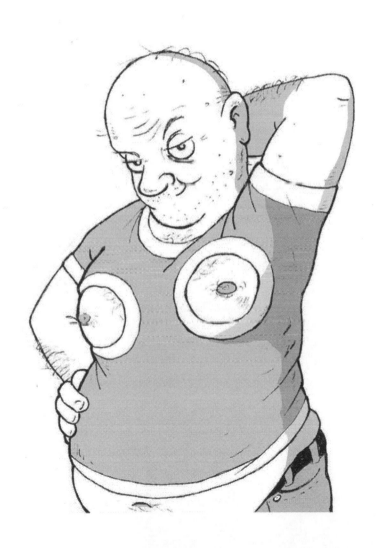

Moob fashions are by and large divided into two distinct groups. Those which seek to conceal or diminish the size of a chap's *'geezer squeezers'* and those that elevate, reveal and revel in the joy of *'chap baps'*. To bounce free or to camouflage one's frontage is of course a personal decision that all of us lucky enough to possess *'fella melons'* must make at one time or another. In this chapter we offer you the garments that perform both tasks without bias or criticism.

The choice is yours and yours alone . . and your other half's of course . . and your work mates . . . anyway . .

The Moob Tube

A classic of simple minimalist design. As popular today as when it first bounced onto our high streets back in the 1970's the Moobtube is both practical and fashionable. Famously worn in the 1980's by TV's Tom Selleck in the now infamous 'accidentally' erased episode of Magnum P.I.

Available in countless styles and colours from floral Hawaiian to battle-ready camouflage prints the Moobtube is here to stay and an essential bit of summer kit for any outgoing moobmeister.

The Peek-a-boo!

Make a definite statement with this cheeky little number!
Not for the shy and retiring among us and certainly
not for cold weather wear. First seen on the
French riviera and lately on the streets of
just about every major European capital
this daring shirt never fails to make a
fella stand out from the crowd!

The Crop Top

A classic unisex look that never goes
out of favour. Tease passers by with
a tantalizing glimpse of moob!
Playful, provocative and fun the
Crop Top says 'Check it out gals coz
I just don't give a damn'! Ideal Summer party wear.

46.

Get it off your chest . . .

Frankie may have said 'Relax' in the
1980's but in the 21st century it's *your*
turn to say 'Check out my chaps!'
Make a definite statement and one hell
of an impact with a Moobmeister slogan
t-shirt! Choose from a fantastic range of
bap-tastic T's available at
www.bookofmoobs.com

Aciiiiiiid!

Prints that accentuate the fuller
figure can be a fella's best friend.
Patterns that compliment and work
with the undulations of one's moobs
are a fashionable and modern way of
using what nature was good enough
to give you to it's fullest advantage!
Mesmerize that special someone
with your hypno-norks!

47.

Not everyone blessed with fella-melons is necessarily keen to show them off to the wider world. Down through the centuries different garments have been devised to minimize or conceal what was once considered an embarrassing imperfection! For every Vivienne Westwood who dares to break the mould with new and provocative creations there are armies of tailors stitching steadily away at more modest designs. Darker colours, looser fitting shirts and multiple layers can all play a part in diverting attention from man boobs. Accessories too can be used to great effect. Is a scarf just there to keep your neck warm or also to dangle down over those bouncing beauties?

In 1891 Parisian tailor Jean-Louis Montgolfier patented his 'Universal Camouflage Weskit'. Initially intended as the last word in life preservers for the French navy Montgolfier quickly recognized the garment's potential and re-marketed it as a gentleman's jacket and chest concealer. After enjoying brief popularity among Paris's sporting set sales of the weskit quickly dwindled as did Mr Montgolfier's finances and in 1896 he was declared bankrupt and committed to the *'Carcassonne Memorial Sanatorium for the Sartorially Baffled'*.

The Waistcoat (or Vest as it is known in the USA) has been with us since it's introduction by King Charles II in 1666. Concerned by the increasing size of his royal 'Monarch Melons' Charles hit upon the idea of an external male corset after one of his many 'un-buttoning' sessions with mistress Nell Gwyn. It remains a favourite method of concealing one's 'oranges' to this day.

Multiple layers have always been a favourite of those seeking to disguise their natural shape. Two or three jumpers and a couple of shirts may obscure the true nature of a fella's figure but the overall effect is often that of a man being swallowed by his knitwear!

In warmer climates the layered approach soon becomes uncomfortable and unhygienic. When faced with a beach holiday scenario there really is very little that the moob conscious chap can do short of staying in his hotel room during daylight hours. One option of course is the Victorian all-in-one bathing suit but wearers should bear in mind that stripes are not kind to those with a fuller figure and a 'Borat' style Mankini should be avoided at all costs!

Chapter Three: Moob History

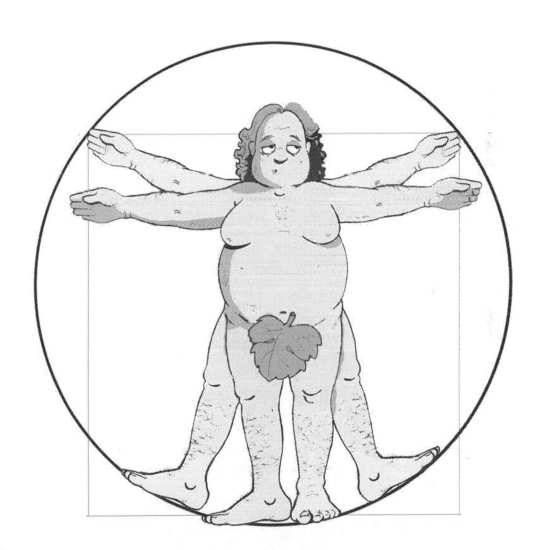

Man boobs are of course as old as history itself. Down through the ages they have always been there, bouncing quietly away as fashions have come and gone, wars have raged and empires have risen and fallen. Despite this omnipresence they have largely been ignored by historians. Why this should be is something of a mystery as the evidence of their rich contribution to human civilisation is all around us. In this chapter we endeavour to put the record straight. The next time you are walking the marbled halls of the British museum or perusing the galleries of the Tate keep an eye open for the many, many 'man-melons' on display!

When primitive man first sought to paint his own likeness onto the walls of his cave the image of the moob was first captured for posterity.

The earliest known examples are found in the Lascaux region of Southern France. 32,000 years old they are a beautiful and fascinating glimpse into the earliest days of our species. Some academics have sought to explain this discovery away as being nothing much more than the depiction of a female hunter. We beg to differ! Decide for yourself.

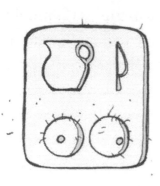

King Juggasese III

Amongst the vast wealth of historical records left to us by the ancient Egyptians are the tomb inscriptions of King Juggasese III. Perhaps a minor pharaoh in some ways (his reign lasted only two and a half months) but still a major player in the 'boy-bosom' department. Certain aspects of Egyptian religious practice and ritual have long been deliberately ignored by western researchers. At the birth of Egyptology in the late 1800's Victorian archeologists simply could not bring themselves to publish some of their more 'fruity' discoveries.

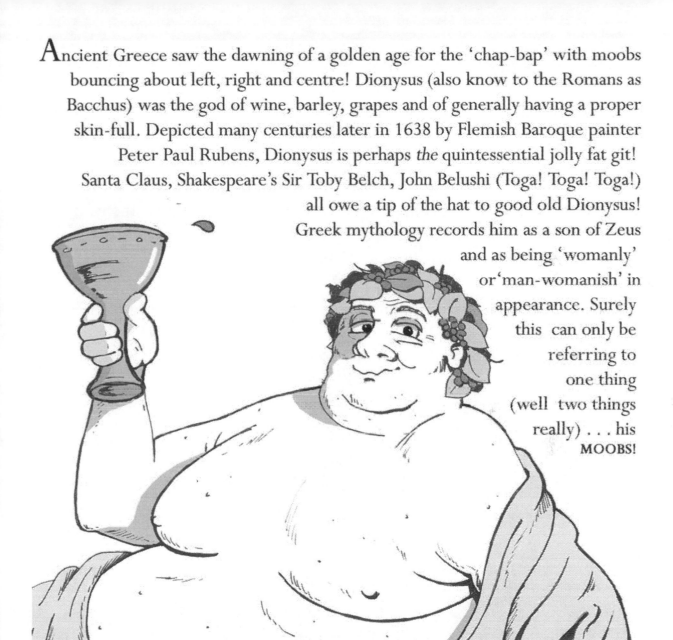

Ancient Greece saw the dawning of a golden age for the 'chap-bap' with moobs bouncing about left, right and centre! Dionysus (also know to the Romans as Bacchus) was the god of wine, barley, grapes and of generally having a proper skin-full. Depicted many centuries later in 1638 by Flemish Baroque painter Peter Paul Rubens, Dionysus is perhaps *the* quintessential jolly fat git! Santa Claus, Shakespeare's Sir Toby Belch, John Belushi (Toga! Toga! Toga!) all owe a tip of the hat to good old Dionysus! Greek mythology records him as a son of Zeus and as being 'womanly' or 'man-womanish' in appearance. Surely this can only be referring to one thing (well two things really) . . . his MOOBS!

Eastern cultures have always been a happy hunting ground for the globe trotting moob-spotter. Asia is packed to the rafters with wonderful statues of the Buddha. Large or small, carved in stone or cast in gold they are simply everywhere! Built during the Tang dynasty (618-907) the Leshan giant Buddha in China is currently believed to be the world's largest but plans for an even bigger one at Maitreya, Kushinagar, Uttar Pradesh State, India will create a bronze statues some five hundred feet tall! This colossal figure will have what must surely be the world's biggest moobs! Each bap will measure an estimated forty feet in width and weigh in at over thirty tons . . . phew!

If ever there was an advertisement for the intoxicating effect that absolute power and massive moobs can have on the fairer sex then King Henry VIII of England was it! Mesmerized by his magnificent royal melons Catherine of Aragon, Anne Boleyn, Jane Seymour, Anne of Cleves, Catherine Howard and Katherine Parr all ignored the obvious dangers of getting 'jiggy' with a tyrannical monster in order to get near to his Tudor Chap-baps.

By all accounts an aggressive egomaniacal drunken lout Henry destroyed the powerful English monasteries, broke with the church of Rome and ended his days as a "putrid, rotting mountain of flesh" . . . still nobody's perfect eh!

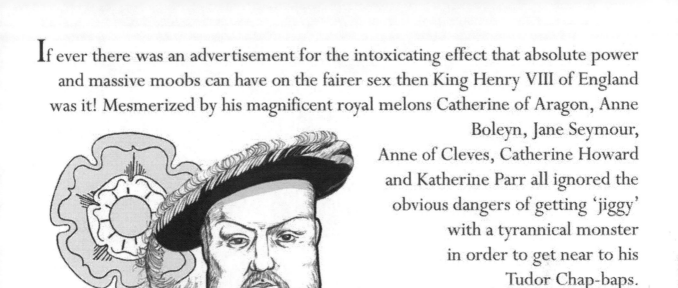

The early 20th century saw a revolution in art and design that fundamentally changed the ways in which we view the world around us. At the forefront of this aesthetic shift were the 'Cubists' Georges Braque and Pablo Picasso. Their radically new approach to painting sent shock waves through the art world that still reverberate to this day! At the heart of Cubist ideology was an attempt to show a painting's subject from multiple view points and angles all on the same picture plane. One of Picasso's lesser known works *'L'homme avec le grand coffre de fumer' (1908)* shows the artist getting to grips with the dimensions of the Le Man boobs. Sacre bleu!

58.

Amid the mountains of man melons that history has shown us one group tower like twin alpine peaks. Their dedication to building and maintaining mammoth amounts of he-vage is second to none. Not content with privately cultivating their Olympian swingers they proudly flaunt them to the world wearing nothing but giant nappies! These super men are of course Japan's legendary Sumo Wrestlers.

Professional Sumo wrestling can trace its origins back as far as 1684 and is believed to have begun as a contest between samurai at the temple of Tomioka Hachiman in Tokyo. Swathed in legend and complex customs Sumo enjoys an almost religious status among its legions of dedicated fans although to many western eyes is essentially two fat gits having a cuddle. Wrestlers work tirelessly to keep their weight up whilst remaining in top athletic condition. This requires simply gargantuan quantities of grub and meal times are really something to behold!

The heaviest ever Sumo was Konishiki Yasokichi. This Hawaiian born behemoth is affectionately known as 'The Dump Truck' and weighed in at an almighty 287 kg (630lb). Check out those Man Boobs - respect!

As the collective girth of western nations continues to swell so too might the esteem in which our moobs are held. We can only hope so. Whereas in decades past the 'body beautiful' has come to mean bulging muscles and waspish waists perhaps future generations will learn to love their moobs as they should! Far from being a sign of gluttony or lack of exercise they may once again come to represent prosperity and success. The obsession with a trimmer figure is after all only a comparatively recent development. Thanks to Coco Channel the late twentieth century saw millions of women desperately tanning their hides into the texture of old shoe leather. Sun-bronzed was the look to have. Now with incidents of skin cancer at record levels we see the fashion start to reverse itself. So too perhaps with the Kate Moss's of this world. Only a few generations ago things were very different. To Victorian eyes the 'must have look' for 'it-girls' was pale and plump! The merry-go-round of fashion spins ever on!

Who knows, in times to come our role models, heroes and even *Super Heroes* may cut a very different and altogether fuller figure!

Chapter Four: Care & Maintenance

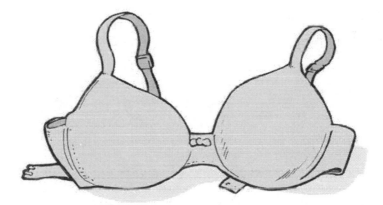

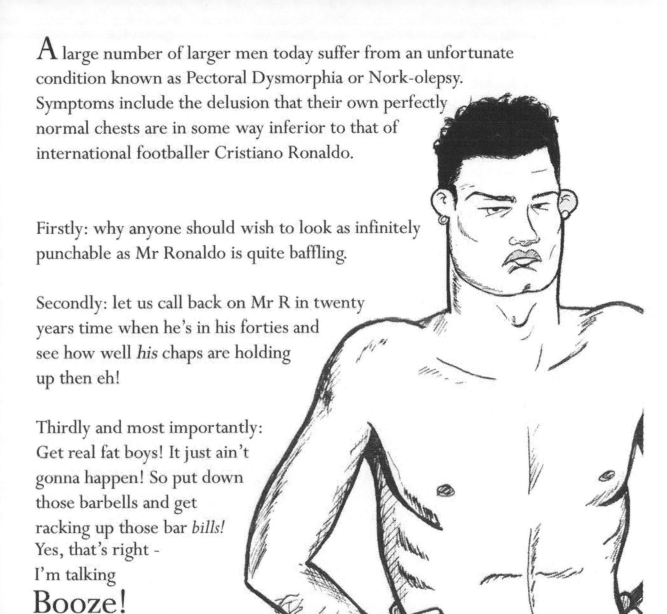

A large number of larger men today suffer from an unfortunate condition known as Pectoral Dysmorphia or Nork-olepsy. Symptoms include the delusion that their own perfectly normal chests are in some way inferior to that of international footballer Cristiano Ronaldo.

Firstly: why anyone should wish to look as infinitely punchable as Mr Ronaldo is quite baffling.

Secondly: let us call back on Mr R in twenty years time when he's in his forties and see how well *his* chaps are holding up then eh!

Thirdly and most importantly: Get real fat boys! It just ain't gonna happen! So put down those barbells and get racking up those bar *bills!* Yes, that's right - I'm talking

Booze!

One of the truly wonderful things about being a Moob meister is that alcohol, if used as part of a calorie uncontrolled diet really can help in the cultivation and maintenance of a healthy he-vage!

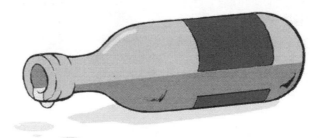

Unbelievable as it may seem, the combination of thousands of empty calories and the almost total physical inertia associated with a good old fashioned ale session really can add vital inches where a chap needs them most - on his baps!

Forget fancy fad diets and quick fixes! The recumbent ingestion of intoxicating liquor will, given time and dedication produce impressive results. *

* Side effects may include memory loss, financial hardship and an urge to sing Karaoke.

Pastimes which involve the raising of one's arms above head height are best avoided as this can lead directly to a firming of the pectoral muscles and eventual loss of moobage! Also strenuous thrusting of the arms to the sides as when performing the breast stroke can be most detrimental and along with *all* other forms of swimming is strongly advised against.

Acceptable sports and pastimes:

Drinking
Television viewing
Sleeping
Cinema going
Card games
Competitive eating
Reading
Listening to the radio
Staring out of the window
Computer games
Snooker/Billiards/Pool (in moderation)
Golf (in moderation)
Darts (also in moderation)
More drinking

Sports and pastimes to be avoided:

Swimming

Football

Rugby

Rugby league

American football

Tennis

Table tennis

Badminton

Squash

All forms of running

Archery

Basketball

Gymnastics

Ice hockey

Karate

Netball

Polo

Frisbee

Volleyball

Cricket

Surfing

Kung Fu

Wii fit

Mountaineering

Hang gliding

Orienteering

Pot Holing

Scuba diving

Water skiing

Skiing

Snow boarding

Ice skating

Roller skating

Cycling

All Olympic sports

Sex*

Boxing

Rowing

Sailing

Salsa dancing

Equestrian events

And anything that involves leaving your armchair.

* Some positions are acceptable. Consult your Kama Sutra or local barmaid.

Not all food stuffs are suitable for moob cultivation. Some 'healthy' foods have been proven to contain potentially life enhancing levels of vitamins and minerals and little or no concentrated fat. As a rule of thumb suitable meals can be divided using the green/brown method. Green for 'no' and brown for 'yes please and can I have seconds?'

Green:
Fruit
Vegetables
Mould
Frogs

Brown:
Chocolate
Meat
Chips
Beer

With all forms of body building a good nutritional regime is key. The Moob-minded amongst us could do well to study the dietary example set by those most bap-tastic of athletes - Sumo wrestlers.

1. Miss out on breakfast. By depriving the body of nutrition after eight hours sleep the metabolic rate is kept low.

2. If you really *must* do some exercise always do it on an empty stomach. This sets the metabolic thermostat to low in order to conserve fuel.

3. Always take a good long nap after eating. Three or four hours should do the trick, the last thing you want to do is go and burn off those burgers!

4. Eat late in the day. Going to bed soon after dinner maximises the calorie/moob conversion ratio.

5. Always eat with other people! Research has shown that a meal eaten in the company of others can be 44 percent larger and contain 30 percent more calories and fat!

6. Always, always, always have dessert. Remember that fruit does not count and that yoghurt is the Swiss word for 'off milk'!

Love your Moobs!

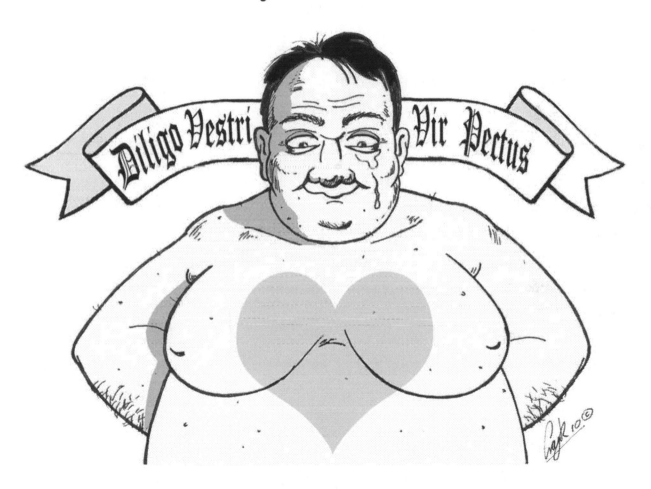

Thanks to Grant, Adam and all the marvellous Moobsters of the world!

Also by Gray K Davis

The Erotic Morris (Ye Olde English Kama Sutra)
www.eroticmorris.com

37166732R00044

Made in the USA
Lexington, KY
20 November 2014